FLOUR POWER
Never Run Out of What You Need

David R. Stokes

FLOUR POWER
Copyright © 2016 David R. Stokes
All rights reserved.
Critical Mass Books
Fairfax, Virginia

ISBN-13: 978-1541118706

For More Information:
 www.expectation.church
Cover Design: Eowyn Riggins
Also By David R. Stokes:
The Shooting Salvationist
Camelot's Cousin
Jack & Dick
November Surprise
Firebrand
Jake & Clara
In the Arena
How To Keep Calm and Carry On
The Simple Life
Got Any Rivers?
The Bothered Butler
Author's Website: www.davidrstokes.com
Amazon Author Page: amazon.com/author/davidstokes

To Brenda Boose, a single mom whose life and faith demonstrate Flour Power every day. She inspires all who know her.

In the Bible Book of First Kings, chapter seventeen,
Pay attention to verses one through sixteen
And if, like Elijah, your life seems sour,
Take a lesson from God's grace in "FlOUR POWER."

You see, Elijah predicted a terrible drought
And food became scarce in the land throughout
But God provided a widow with flour
A minimal provision just right for that hour

Then a miracle happened all by God's grace
As water and food was provided with haste
From a handful of flour and oil in a jar
An endless provision appeared from afar

Sure death was averted that very minute
For when God is in it, we will always win it
And in everything that God leads us to
He will insure that we make it through

By seeking God through faith we can surely see
Jesus' promises fulfilled in Matthew 6:33
Blessings are abundant as to God we draw near
Obedient faith will conquer human fear

God provides for our needs if we are obedient
Faith is the key and the main ingredient
Our extremity is HIS opportunity
And in response to fear we have immunity

Our response in life when circumstances seem dire
Is to activate our faith and obedience through the fire
Obedient faith activates supernatural power
So, take a lesson from the scriptures concerning "FLOUR POWER"

— Rev. Howard "Ike" Hendershot, 11/17/16

FLOUR POWER
Never Run Out of What You Need

Back in the late 1960s, a time defined by the counterculture movement in America, people talked about "flower power," a term coined by a poet named Allen Ginsburg. Think bell bottoms, flower crowns, San Francisco, hippies, and Haight-Ashbury.

Far out, man.

Nearly 3,000 years ago in Israel's Northern Kingdom, then ruled by a king named Ahab and his infamous wife, Jezebel, a different kind of "Flour Power" saved a single mother and her son from starvation during a time of famine. This is a power that is very much available to us today, and it can revolutionize our lives.

The story features one of the most intriguing characters in scripture. His name was Elijah—a bold and fiery prophet of God. He appeared suddenly on the scene out of obscurity, seeming to come from nowhere. He made an impact on his times, a particularly idolatrous period in Israel's history.

Queen Jezebel was the personification of evil. She became a persistent metaphor for evil later in scripture and still holds that distinction to this day. Born in Phoenicia, a region north of Israel, she was completely immersed in its pagan culture and its gods. Under her influence, there developed a syncretic mishmash of religious ideas that became widespread in the culture. Then, as happens when there is a time of need, God raised up his own one-man "counter-culture"—Elijah the prophet.

Elijah was an original. Long after he lived and preached, he was the prophet all others would be compared to—the gold standard of preachers. John the Baptist was compared to Elijah. So was Jesus. It was meant as a compliment. It would be like somebody in our time saying, "This man is the next Billy Graham."

Abruptly, Elijah entered King Ahab's court with a bold and provocative message—like John the Baptist would do with Herod centuries later. Elijah prophesied that because of their disobedience, because of their idolatry, there would be judgment from God. Under Jezebel's sinister influence, the people had begun to worship Baal, the supreme god of the Canaanites. They considered him the "giver of life," with absolute control over man and nature. They also saw Baal as the god of fertility. The people began to offer sacrifices for fair weather, healthy crops, and victory in battle. They demonstrated their devotion through vile depravity, including ritualistic self-mutilation, acts of prostitution, and even human sacrifice.

Baal represents the idolatrous "gold standard" of false gods in the Old Testament. Even Jesus once, when referring to Satan as *Beelzebub*, was using a form of the word *Baal*. This kind of "worship" in Israel was the epitome of evil and demonic activity.

This was the spiritual climate in Israel when Elijah appeared on the scene. He said: *"As the Lord, the God of Israel lives, whom I serve, there will be neither dew nor rain in the next few years except at my word."* (I Kings 17:1 NIV) A drought, accompanied by famine was coming. What an audacious statement! With his words, Elijah showed his defiance and contempt for both the crown and the first couple's so-called "god."

Jezebel was not happy. And in those days people probably said something like, "If Jezebel ain't happy, nobody's happy." She became the model for Lewis Carroll's queen of hearts and wanted Elijah killed. So God instructed Elijah to run. The prophet is directed to a ravine, where a brook named Kerith flowed. He then told Elijah that he had arranged for some ravens to feed him.

Ravens seem like an odd choice as a food delivery mechanism. They were "unclean" according to both Jewish law and custom. But God reminded Elijah— and us—there are times when he will use unusual, messy, and even unclean things to help his people along the way.

As God promised, the ravens fed Elijah by bringing him bread and meat, and because God had hidden him by a stream where there was plenty of fresh water. But eventually, the brook started to recede and Elijah found himself in a critical situation. First Kings, chapter 17, verse 7 says: *"Some time later the brook dried up because there had been no rain in the land. Then the word of the Lord came to him...".*

Think about that timeline. The brook dried up, and *then* the word of the Lord came. Most of us today are so wired for convenience and predictability that we want to know the next step long before the brook dries up. We cry out for plan B long before plan A has played out. We like to think several moves ahead, like good chess players. But it is usually an exercise in futility and frustration. Perhaps Elijah had been praying, "Lord, the water level is going down. This thing is going to dry up, so either you are going to give me the signal and say it is going to rain, or you will tell me the next step." Makes sense, right? But that is not the way God works most of the time.

Every great step of faith in our lives will contain, by necessity, a measure of desperation. We actually learn more about spiritual power when we are between the rock and the hard place. It was not as the brook was drying up that God said, "In about a month you need to make your plans." No, it was after the brook dried up that Elijah heard once again from God: *"Go at once to Zarephath in the region of Sidon and stay there. I have directed a widow there to supply you with food."* (I Kings 17:9 NIV)

This is a fascinating directive from the Lord. First of all, Zarephath was about 100 miles away. And even more interesting is the fact that Sidon was the home region of Jezebel and her pagan worship. Remember, Elijah was a wanted man. That was why God had hidden him in the ravine. Now he seems to be telling his preacher, "I want you to go out in broad daylight, and I want you to travel many miles into that region. I have somebody there." He was sending Elijah from safety to peril.

Jesus talked about this: *"I assure you that there were many widows in Israel in Elijah's time, when the sky was shut for three and a half years and there was a severe famine throughout the land. Yet Elijah was not sent to any of them, but to a widow in Zarephath in the region of Sidon."* (Luke 4:25-26 NIV)

What can we learn from this?

Where God leads, God feeds.

If God leads us, He is going to feed us. If God leads us, He is going to fund us. Since my childhood I have tried my best to follow the leadership of God. As often as I have allowed, God has led me. David said, "I have been young and I have been old, and I have never seen the righteous forsaken nor his seed begging bread." God provides.

Many Sunday mornings my wife and I have that all-important conversation, "Where are we going to go to eat after church?" Not, "How are we going to come up with food?" Not, "Who are we going to try to hang out with and see if they might buy the preacher a free meal?" No. God has taken care of us. I sometimes wonder how that has happened, and I often think about some of the times when we did not know how we were going to make ends meet. But we learned long ago about how God blends *leading* with *feeding*.

Don't worry. In the Sermon on the Mount, Jesus addressed this:

"Therefore I tell you, do not worry about your life, what you will eat or drink; or about your body, what you will wear. Is not life more than food, and the body more than clothes? Look at the birds of the air; they do not sow or reap or store away in barns, and yet your heavenly Father feeds them. Are you not much more valuable than they? Can any one of you by worrying add a single hour to your life?

"And why do you worry about clothes? See how the flowers of the field grow. They do not labor or spin. Yet I tell you that not even Solomon in all his splendor was dressed like one of these. If that is how God clothes the grass of the field, which is here today and tomorrow is thrown into the fire, will he not much more clothe you—you of little faith? So do not worry, saying, 'What shall we eat?' or 'What shall we drink?' or 'What shall we wear?' For the pagans run after all these things, and your heavenly Father knows that you need them. But seek first his kingdom and his righteousness, and all these things will be given to you as well. Therefore do not worry about tomorrow, for tomorrow will worry about itself. Each day has enough trouble of its own." (Matthew 6:25-34 NIV)

The context of his comments was the discussion of the larger issue of not making earthly treasures the main thing. Rust will corrupt our automobiles, moths will eat our garments, and thieves can ransack our homes, but we are to trust in God—not the national economy.

We need things—there is no shame or judgment in that. But this should not be where our heart is.

Seek *Him* first, *His* kingdom, *His* righteousness. What is His kingdom? Whatever is important to the King is his kingdom. Wherever He rules is His kingdom. So seek what He values, and God will take care of the rest. I am living proof of that, and so are many others of you reading this simple book. It is supernatural. It makes no sense. There is no logic to it. But it's quite real.

Sometimes an individual will come to their extended family and say, "God is calling me to the mission field." And instead of encouragement the response is, "Well, how are you going to live? What are you going to do? You mean you are going to live in a hut, and you are not going to have any electricity and running water?"

Where God leads, God feeds. If God is in it, He will feed you. He will take care of you. There is no doubt about it. Take it to the bank, because even if the bank fails, God never will.

Whatever God calls us to, He will get us through.

It does not always feel like this though, does it? I am

not saying it is going to be pain free. Elijah's journey from Kerith to Zarephath, 100 miles through enemy territory, was incredibly risky from a human standpoint. But he reasoned, "God has called me to something. He is going to get me through this."

Think about the story from Genesis chapter twenty-two about Abraham being tested and asked to take Isaac to the mountain for sacrifice. According to the Book of Hebrews, Abraham reckoned by faith that even if Isaac died on that sacrificial altar, God would be able to bring him back from the dead. God had already promised him a great family through Isaac. So when God told him that Isaac must be sacrificed, his faith-response was "God is doing something I do not understand. But I'm going to trust Him, because if Isaac dies, he will have to come back from the dead."

When God is in it, he will get you through it. It may be painful. It may hurt. There may be problems. Nobody goes through life without a series of difficulties and challenges. Babe Ruth was a great ballplayer, but did you know that for many years he also held the record for striking out? You can fail 67 percent of the time in baseball and still make the Hall of Fame. Now that is a great job. I would say the only thing better is being a weatherman.

God wants to lead us. He wants to take us to the next part of our journey in His will. Our job is to focus on the big picture and let God take care of the rest. Our tendency is to spend too much time analyzing. There is an old saying, "Analyze, analyze, paralyze." If we spend too much time analyzing, the only result we can expect is paralysis. And then we miss out on God's best for us.

The scriptures tell the story in I Kings chapter seventeen. *"So he went to Zarephath."* Elijah was obedient. *"When he came to the town gate, a widow was there gathering sticks."* He had no way of knowing if this was the particular widow he was to contact. It was not like a light shone down. She is just another desperate widow and single mom. *"He called to her and asked, 'Would you bring me a little water in a jar so I may have a drink?'"* as was customary in their culture. *"As she was going to get it, he called, 'And bring me, please, a piece of bread.'"* Elijah is testing the waters. She answers, *"As surely as the Lord your God lives..."*

Scripture gives us this dialogue between the two characters and there are certain things that are safe to infer from what we see in this passage. Perhaps Elijah had communicated with her or perhaps because of his reputation she knew that he was a man of God. We can see by her statement, *"As surely as the Lord your God lives..."* that she was a woman of faith. It may have been revelation from God, because God had already said, *"I have commanded someone to supply your need."*

"'As surely as the Lord your God lives,' she replied, 'I do not have any bread—only a handful of flour in a jar and a little olive oil in a jug. I am gathering a few sticks to take home and make a meal for myself and my son, that we may eat it—and die.'"

How would you like to hear that from someone? "Well, I would bring you a piece of bread, but I only have enough for me and my son, and we are going to eat it and die." Wow.

I have read this account for many years with an image of someone my mother-in-law's age, a woman in her early eighties, in my mind, but she is a young mother. She has a son - a *young* son. This is probably a widow in her twenties. Elijah has the audacity to say to this single mother, *"Bring me some bread,"* but she does not hesitate to give him a dose of reality.

Think of it this way: You are a single mom not even thirty years old. I approach you, sit down and you say, "How are you doing, Pastor?" I respond, "Would you get me a sandwich?" Maybe you say, "Sure, I can do that for you," while thinking, *typical helpless man*.

What if you said, "I only have a couple slices of bread, and things are not going that well. My son and I have enough to eat, and when we eat this we do not know where our next meal is coming from. We are probably just going to die." My response to that is probably not going to be, "I don't care. I want a sandwich." I am probably going to say, "Don't worry about it. Let me buy some food for you and your son."

But that is not what is going on here. Why? Because God is doing something. He is teaching something. God often uses the unlikely to accomplish great things.

He is using this single mom, this widow, to do something phenomenal.

She is going to discover *flour power*.

God has chosen a single mom, a woman at her wits end. No money, no food, no prospects, a child to care for, nobody to care for her in the midst of an economic disaster. There seems to be no hope.

"But" is one of my favorite words in the Bible, it is a conjunction that always makes a difference. *But God* chose to make a difference. He loves to use the foolish things to confound the wise. The next time you think, "I do not have much to offer the Lord. I do not have any talents, any skills. I do not have any resources." God is asking for your *heart*. Start *where* you are. Start with *who* you are and *what* you have, and let God take it and break it and use it for His glory.

I recently had an example of this in my own life. I am the oldest of three boys, and my brother Greg is two years younger than I am. Greg was the middle child, and he always seemed to be in trouble. Honestly, probably much of it was because I talked him into things. As kids, our Dad never spanked us, he just prayed for us and quoted Scripture and wept. Not my Mom. She was spontaneous (read: watch out!) and did not "spare the rod."

One of my favorite stories from when we were kids is when both Greg and I were in trouble for something. I took responsibility and accepted what was coming to me. But not Greg. He ran. He always ran, as if he was going to out-run our mother. My mom was just five-foot-two, 95 pounds, but she was strong. Think the Shakespearean quote, "Though she be but little, she is fierce!" I can still see it all as clear as day. Greg crawled under her bed. My mom crawled under the bed after him. He came out the other side. She came out. It was twice as bad for him. Greg was not smart.

Greg dropped out of high school when he was in the eleventh grade, without telling my parents. He just quit going and in time got involved in juvenile criminal activities. He never had a record, because his partner in crime was the son of a local politician (always choose the right partner). As a result, nothing was ever prosecuted.

By the time Greg turned eighteen, my dad had had enough and said, "You are not going to be a bum. Pick a branch of the service. You are not going to live under my roof." So Greg joined the navy, thinking it would be an easier life than living under Dad's roof.

Greg rebelled against the things of God and ended up away from church for many years. Classic preacher's kid. My dad was old school and Greg wanted no part of it. As kids, my father had no problem calling us out when we were acting up in church, even during his preaching he would stop and say from the pulpit, "David and Greg, you stop that right now!" It happened so smoothly we thought it was Scripture.

Once, and I emphasize *once*, he made Greg come up and sit on the platform right behind him. That was a big mistake, because Greg made faces at us the entire time. It was pretty funny, well it was funny until my dad found out after the service what had been happening.

Back in his early 20s, Greg was stationed in Portsmouth, Virginia. After being invited to church by a friend, he got saved. Talk about transformation. God completely changed his life. So much so that when Greg got out of the navy, he went off to Bible college, trained for the ministry and was ordained in 1984. He eventually followed my dad as the pastor of the church where dad had served as senior pastor, the church where I was ordained in 1977.

As I mentioned, Greg was a high school dropout. But years later he was elected to the school board in our home town, even though all he had was a GED. In fact, he eventually became the president of that school board. Years later, when he moved to Connecticut where he began to minister, they awarded him his diploma—something he should have received in 1976. That was pretty cool.

Greg has always gotten involved in civic affairs. He is different from me. He loves meetings. He loves being at a table with a group of people, everybody sharing their thoughts and ideas. He just loves meetings. I on the other hand, do not like meetings. At all. I do not have the attention span or patience they require. If you have ever spoken to me you know this is true because when I talk to you, after three minutes you know I am gone. Just wandered off in my mind, I have mentally checked out.

In the November 2016 elections, Greg was elected to the state legislature in Connecticut, the first Republican in his district. I was very proud of him. Recently my grandsons were staying with us. Grayson was picking on Sawyer and I said, "You'd better be careful. Your little brother may grow up to become a congressman. Mine did." If you had told someone back in the 70s, "Greg Stokes is going to be a political leader in the state of Connecticut," they'd have said, "Yeah, sure."

Clearly his journey has been different from mine, though we are both pastors. Never think God cannot change you or use you. Do not let other people's opinions of you determine your path. Focus on God's opinion of you. Do not worry about what anybody else thinks.

I think we can all agree opinions can be flawed and first impressions are not always accurate. Over the years, I have picked some losers. "Oh, that is the guy there. He has so much talent. Look at her. So much talent." And yet too often they have been the ones who have crashed and burned, and instead some smart-mouthed kid who could not connect two sentences becomes the one God uses. Our extremity is His opportunity. When we get to the extreme, that is God's opportunity.

Now listen to what the story says.

"Elijah said to her, 'Do not be afraid. Go home and do as you have said. But first make a small loaf of bread for me from what you have and bring it to me, and then make something for yourself and your son.'" But *first*, and *then*. If you take care of yourself first before doing what God wants you to do, you miss it.

But first, and then.

"For this is what the Lord, the God of Israel, says: 'The jar of flour will not be used up and the jug of oil will not run dry until the day the Lord sends rain on the land.' She went away and did as Elijah had told her. So there was food every day..." According to the record, he stayed there quite a long time. There were probably 2,000 meals, a lot of biscuits prepared from that bottomless jar of *flour power*.

"...every day for Elijah and for the woman and her family. For the jar of flour was not used up and the jug of oil did not run dry, in keeping with the word of the Lord spoken by Elijah."

Flour power. Real-life wonder bread. I cannot explain to you the number of times and the number of ways that God brought my family through difficult times. We have a nice life now. We live in a nice place, we have a nice car, we have a good health plan.

None of our kids, however, were born on a health plan. No church provided health care coverage for us until I had been pastoring for more than ten years. We always had to make payments to the hospital. We never figured out how we were going to do that. We could not go out to eat. Occasionally I would pray that I would get the opportunity to make a hospital visit on Sunday, because on Sundays the cafeteria at the local hospital provided a discount for pastors and I could feed my family. "Taking you out today, honey. We are going to the hospital cafeteria!" How about that? Big spender.

That is how we lived. Over the years God has changed that. There were many times I do not know how we did it. I do not even remember how we paid the hospital off when Brenda was born. I know we did, but I do not remember how. Every time I reached down into that jar, God had something there. Logically, it shouldn't have been there, but I had learned to live on *flour power*.

Obedient faith is the best response to fear.

God says, "Do not be afraid." But that single mom was afraid. Would you be afraid? Of course you would. If I were to say, "I know you are starving. I know your son has not had anything to eat. I know you have your needs, but I still want you to take care of me first." That would be audacious. That would be ugly. People would say, "That is typical preacher entitlement." But wait. God was doing something. He was teaching this woman a principle. Yes, she was afraid. You would be too. But, the right response is, "I will do it, Pastor, because I believe you are sensitive to the leadership of the Lord, even though it still doesn't make sense."

Are you afraid of something right now? The best antidote for fear is to interrupt that pattern immediately. Change your body language. Get up and do something good for someone. Give something to someone. This can chase fear away because you are refusing to be paralyzed. Move. Move forward. Move forward in obedience and faith.

Obedient faith activates supernatural power.

That's the essence of flour power. How did God do it? I have no clue. How did the Lord turn the loaves and the fishes into enough to feed more than 5,000 people? How did the Lord turn the water into wine? How did he part the Red Sea? How did he provide manna from heaven? I cannot explain any of that to you scientifically.

I simply leave ample room in my thinking for the supernatural.

What God is saying is, "If you obey Me, seek Me first and every time you reach down thinking there is nothing left, you will find that it is not empty. You will have enough to take care of your need." This is triggered when you push back on fear and say, "I am going to do something good, and I am going to become a giver rather than a taker."

Many years ago there was an entertainer named Amos

Jacobs. He grew up in the 1920s in the Detroit area. When he was about ten years old he got a job selling what we from the Midwest call *pop* in a theater. He caught the show business bug. He wanted to be a singer. He had a pretty good voice, and he had a pretty quick wit about him. By the time he was sixteen he was pursuing his dream.

His mother was a devout, churchgoing, God-fearing woman who faithfully took the kids to church. She didn't want her boy to be a showman, she wanted him to start a business, to do something with his life. But his mind was made up, and he would not be deterred.

During one gig he met a girl. They eventually married and started a family, living hand-to-mouth, moving from place to place. Finally, Amos got a break and a good job at a famous club in Detroit. Things were looking up until the day he came home and told his pregnant wife, that he had gotten his notice that day. The club was closing, and he no longer had a job.

He had a child on the way and just $7.85 in his pocket.

The next day was Sunday and he and his wife went to church. Amos prayed, "God, please take care of us." The offering basket was passed and he thought, "I will put something in the basket, I guess." So he pulled a dollar bill from his pocket. Then he felt that God was speaking to him and saying, "I want all seven dollars." So he reached back into his pocket and pulled out the other six dollar bills and put it all in the basket. I am pretty sure his wife looked at him and her face probably said, "Seriously?"

Amos walked out of that church with 85 cents in his pocket and no prospect of a job. He prayed, "Lord, I have done this, but you have to take care of me." The next morning, he got a telephone call. It was an agent who had a radio commercial for him that paid $75. He started shouting for joy. He prayed, "Lord, you keep meeting my needs, I will put you first, and I will do something significant for you, whatever it is you want."

His career started to take off, and he soon decided that Amos Jacobs was not a real celebrity-style name, so he took the first names of two of his brothers as his show business name. He had a brother named Danny and another brother named Thomas. Danny. Thomas.

Danny Thomas eventually had a dream to build a hospital for children in need, those with life threatening illnesses considered lost causes, where doctors could do research. In 1958, he broke ground in Memphis, Tennessee, for what is now St. Jude's hospital. My wife sends them support on a regular basis. They do good work.

Do you know where that great institution of healing came from? It came from a man who learned how to give. He did not wait until he was a success to become a giver. *Becoming a giver made him a success.* He did not wait until he was making millions. He did not wait until he was Danny Thomas on *Make Room for Daddy*. He did not wait until he was producing *The Andy Griffith Show*, *The Dick Van Dyke Show*, and so many others. He did not wait. He discovered *Flour Power* when he had only $7.85 in his pocket, a pregnant wife, and no job. The little he had, he gave to God. He put God first, by faith, and it revolutionized his life.

One of the greatest lessons to learn in life is to stop being a taker and start being a giver. You say, "Pastor, you are just trying to raise money for the church." I will tell you what. All churches have needs, but if you think that is all this is about, then I challenge you to take 90 days and give a tithe to St. Jude's or some other worthy cause. I believe the local church is where your tithe ought to be, but I believe giving is giving, and the principle works whenever and wherever faithfully applied. God wants you to be do-gooders and givers. This is how we can see *flour power* up close and personal.

Isn't it time you stopped living on will-power, or political power, or cultural power and started to live on *flour power*? When you put God first, every time you go to the cupboard there will be something there. It just happens.

It's like this cool miracle that happens at my house. I drop things right where I use them. Take my socks off and leave them right there. Take off my shoes and leave them right there. I come back a little while later and they are gone. Just…gone. It's amazing. Some force , some power has taken the things I have discarded and put them in their appropriate place. Every once in a while the socks will stay for a while. It is like the *Everybody Loves Raymond* suitcase episode. It is a test to see how long it is going to be.

Of course, the "force" is my wife. She picks up after me.

This is funny analogy, I suppose (although Karen doesn't always laugh about it), but if we cast off our things toward God, all our cares, all our worries—and become givers—God will pick up the burdens we've discarded and handle them.

> *"Give all your worries and cares to God, for He cares about you."* — I Peter 5:7 (New Living Translation)

Become a person who gives. Don't worry about the consequences.

If God puts it on your heart to do something good for something or someone, do it. You may think, "I do not know what is going to happen, because I have a lot of issues in my life." Trust me, God will come in and clean up after you. He will pick it all up and put it all together. He will hang it up just the right way, military style. He will shine the shoes. He will do everything. Why? *Flour power.*

If your cupboard is getting bare and you are going through something that is difficult and you are having a hard time seeing how it is going to work out, stop trying to figure it out. Stop where you are. Do not make the mistake too many people make. "As soon as I get my act together, I will put God first." No! You will never get your act together until you put God first. When you put God first; he will help you get your act together.

Do something with what you have. Trust God for what you don't have.

That's *flour power*.

THE BOTHERED BUTLER
Moving from Burden to Breakthrough

THE FASCINATING MEMOIRS of a man named Nehemiah are as relevant to us today as they were when they were written nearly 2,500 years ago. The biblical writings contain timeless lessons about life and leadership.

He was an ordinary man. No pedigree. No life-long preparation. No burning ambition to be a leader or agent of change. But that all changed one day. It changed because he asked a simple question.

First, some background and context.

I love the venerable eighteenth-century hymn, *"Come Thou Fount of Every Blessing,"* written in 1757 by Robert Robinson, an English Methodist pastor. It has a very honest and haunting phrase in its final refrain: *"Prone to wander, Lord, I feel it; prone to leave the God I love."*

It's a reminder that we all have a tendency to wind down and wander off. It's part of our nature. The prophet Isaiah said, *"All we like sheep have gone astray; we have turned—every one—to his own way; and the Lord has laid on him the iniquity of us all."* Sin is about wandering, and that's the biblical story of the nation of Israel. In spite of all of their blessings, all of the promises, even experiencing the Promised Land, they wandered, and they had to go through various seasons of regrouping, rebooting, and restoration. Or we might call it: *Revival.*

We need moments of renewal because of this natural tendency to wander. We see it throughout scripture, so we ought to be able to identify with it. First Corinthians tells us in chapter ten that those things in the Old Testament were written for us in this age. The powerful stories are examples to us. We learn from them.

Or at least we should.

There came a time when the children of Israel wanted a king so they could be like all the other nations. They got Saul. He looked the part and loved the role. But before long, it all went to his head and Saul turned his back on God. So God anointed David to be his ultimate replacement. David was a sterling young man. He was even described as being "a man after God's own heart." But later in life, David gave into his own "prone to wander" tendencies and messed up his life and family big time. As a result of that, the scriptures tell us, *"the sword would not depart from his house."*

The die was cast.

David's son and successor, Solomon, built the great temple in Jerusalem. But after Solomon was gone, there was a split in the kingdom between the north and south. The northern kingdom was comprised of ten tribes. It was known as Israel from that point on. The southern kingdom included the remaining two tribes. It was known as Judah. Judah endured longer than Israel. The Assyrians decimated the Northern Kingdom around 722 BC. God had warned them judgment was coming to Jerusalem and Judah. He sent prophets like Jeremiah to warn the people. He promised Judah a 70-year exile in captivity.

One of the great plot points about Scripture is that it explains both history and the future. These two elements are crucial to our understanding of the events in the Bible and what is happening today. The Bible and history concur and tell us the exile occurred in 586 BC. The Babylonians, led by Nebuchadnezzar, came and ransacked Jerusalem and took the children of Israel into bondage. In fact, the book of *Lamentations* was written as a funeral dirge about the decimation of Jerusalem. As the 70-year period of chastisement was coming to a close, God began to move in the hearts of unlikely persons to fulfill his word to bring them back into the land.

Hundreds of years before Christ, a Persian king called Cyrus the Great rose to power. All of the great leaders in Persian (modern day Iran) history have wanted to trace their lineage back to Cyrus. He was a very dynamic and powerful man. Cyrus issued a decree at the end of the 70 years to allow the migration of the Jews back to Jerusalem in fulfillment of prophecy.

God used an Iranian to do that. A Persian. These nations are constantly in the news today. Josephus, the Jewish historian who wrote the *Antiquities of the Jews*, declared definitively that when Cyrus came across a reference to his name in a prophecy written 150 years *before* he was born, he was convinced that he was unique and he should act for the Jewish people. That prophet was Isaiah, writing in about 740 BC. The name *Cyrus* is mentioned at the end of chapter 44 and the beginning of chapter 51. This was before there *was* a Cyrus. The passage reads, *"I will raise up Cyrus."* So when Cyrus became king of Persia and saw his own name in a prophecy written 150 years or so before he was born, he made the decree to begin the homeward migration of the Jewish people. It was a classic example of biblical prophecy influencing current events and history.

There's an interesting footnote in history. In 1948, we saw the creation of the modern nation state of Israel. Harry Truman was the president of the United States at that time and not doing too well in the polls. In fact, there was a popular saying about him at the time: "To err is Truman." The man was not very popular. But Truman had a friend named Eddie Jacobson, with whom he had owned a clothing store in Missouri years earlier.

Eddie Jacobson was a Jewish man. He was persuaded by some who were advocating for a Jewish homeland in Palestine to try to influence his friend. So he went to the White House to lobby his former business partner. He was successful.

At midnight on May 14, 1948, David Ben-Gurion

declared the establishment of the new state of Israel in Tel Aviv. Eleven minutes later, the first nation to recognize the fragile new nation was the United States of America under the leadership of President Truman. It was a key moment, because in order for something to happen, there had to be affirmation from other nations. Without the support of Truman and the United States, Israel as a nation would have lasted only a few days.

Truman had grown up in a Baptist Sunday school back home in Missouri. He loved history and he knew the Bible. Several years later, well after he left office, he was invited to speak at the Jewish Theological Seminary in New York City. He was introduced as a modern-day Cyrus who had helped take the Jews back into their homeland. Truman jumped up from his seat and said, "I'm not like Cyrus; I *am* Cyrus." Clearly, when Harry Truman signed that document, he did so directly thinking of Cyrus, the king of Persia, issuing that decree 2,500 years earlier.

So the Jews started going back to their homeland. Let's follow the timeline. After the decree from Cyrus, it took roughly one hundred years before Nehemiah became a major player. Actually, for the first 85 years after that famous edict there was little change. Then we come to the story told in the book of Ezra. He recorded the Jews rebuilding the temple—the center of the nation's religious life.

Fast forward another dozen years and we meet

Nehemiah. He was in Persia and served as butler to Artaxerxes I. It was a very powerful position. One of his jobs was to be the cupbearer, a food taster; a role much more intense than you may think. It was not simply a matter of "taste the food to see if it is salty or sweet." Nehemiah's job was to taste the king's food to see if it was poisoned. It was only after Nehemiah had tasted the dishes that the king himself would then eat.

That's trust.

That was the story of the nation of Israel up to that point. Even though they had been sent back into the land, they still had not learned crucial lessons, and it seemed they never would because they were "prone to wander."

Let's look closely at the first few verses from the Memoirs of Nehemiah:

"The words of Nehemiah son of Hakaliah: In the month of Kislev in the twentieth year..." This places it toward the end of November, beginning of December, likely in the year 444 BC. *"...while I was in the citadel of Susa* [in Persia, modern-day Iran], *Hanani, one of my brothers* [his physical brother] *came from Judah with some other men, and I questioned them about the Jewish remnant that had survived the exile, and also about Jerusalem."* (Nehemiah 1:1-2 NIV)

Now a little plot point here—Nehemiah had never actually seen Jerusalem. All of the events he knew about had happened long before he was born. He was born in exile, most likely in Persia. But he had stayed connected to his heritage and was clearly familiar with the writings of the Law and Prophets.

The Book of Nehemiah represents the very end point of history in the Old Testament. In other words, it takes it to the *very end* of the Old Testament, chronologically. All the events that follow in our English Bible, all the Prophets, Psalms, Proverbs, etc., had already been written and lived out prior to Nehemiah's memoir. Nehemiah came on the scene at that particular point, and he was curious about events back in Jerusalem.

"They said to me, 'Those who survived the exile and are back in the province are in great trouble and disgrace. The wall of Jerusalem is broken down, and its gates have been burned with fire.'" That's not a very good report. *"When I heard these things, I sat down and wept. For some days I mourned and fasted and prayed before the God of heaven."* (Nehemiah 1:3-4 NIV)

This was the key moment in Nehemiah's life. It was also a key moment in human history. His memoirs talk about rebuilding the wall of Jerusalem from the rubble. But the story isn't just about a building. The story becomes a metaphor about building or rebuilding anything worthwhile in our lives.

I want to share with you some lessons about building a compelling future in your life along God's lines. And I want to talk about how all of us need to be involved in building the work of God for the Kingdom of God. Not brick and mortar, not property, not geography, but in the sense that we are the building blocks God uses to build His church. Peter told us in his writings, "Jesus is the chief cornerstone" and we as the church are called "lively" or "living stones." We are molded together by God putting us together. It is a powerful and rich metaphor.

My father grew up learning the brick and stonemason trade from his stepfather. Later, his brothers had a company—"Stokes Brothers Construction"—and they built houses and churches in the Detroit, Michigan area. I myself never learned the trade, but I've seen my father as a stonemason taking stone and building something out of all of these rugged and oddly-shaped rocks. Somehow he made them all come together to make something beautiful.

Whether it is brick by brick or stone by stone, God is building us into a habitation He can use. Think of the word *edify*. I want to be edified. The Bible teaches us the church should edify. When they repaired the National Cathedral in Washington, DC after the earthquake a few years ago, they described it as an *edifice*. It's a beautiful edifice. It's a building. *Edify* is the word *building*.

To *edify* is to build up.

The job of the church is building people up. So yes, there is a collective element, but there is also an individual element. As a pastor, I am to help those under my teaching grow. They may not always like everything I say, and there may be a bit of a prod or a kick at times, but it is my responsibility to challenge them to grow to be stronger along the lines God has established and according to God's plan—to build up, to edify. This is how we build a compelling future.

One November night back in 1970 in Dearborn Heights, Michigan, I was sitting in a church service. I was fourteen years old and listening to a great preacher who has since gone home to be with the Lord, a wonderful man of God, Dr. Howard Sears. That night, he repeated over and over again something a British missionary named William Carey said back around the time of the American Revolution.

"Expect great things from God; attempt great things for God."

I have used that statement many times in my life and ministry. It is tied into the very moment when I sensed God's call on my life. I have been on that trajectory in that role, in a sense, ever since that night.

It is the main reason I led our local congregation in Fairfax to adopt the name, *"EXPECTATION CHURCH."* We want to expect great things *from* God, and we want to attempt great things *for* God. I want you to see great things happen along God's lines. Not just what *we* think would be great, because many times what we think is great is not what God thinks is great, and what God thinks is great is not what we think is great. I want us to be bold enough, like Nehemiah was, to attempt great things for God.

When we think of walls in the modern day our first thought is maybe the Berlin Wall and the rejoicing when Reagan spoke those iconic words at Brandenburg Gate; "Mr. Gorbachev, tear down this wall." The fall of the Berlin wall is significant for many reasons, not least of which because it was a wall that was designed to keep something in, not keep something out.

It was a wall that became a metaphor for tyranny.

In the ancient world, cities had walls for very specific reasons. Cities without walls were particularly vulnerable and did not survive very long. They were particularly exposed and constantly at risk of invasion from their enemies.

First of all, walls defined the *base* and the *sphere* of their city. It defined their territory. It defined who they were. Think of the walls of Jerusalem, the walls of Jericho, and others. If you had the right kind of walls, your city was impenetrable. It was insurmountable, and a military opponent had to find another way to defeat you.

Nehemiah asked, *"How is it going in Jerusalem, Hanani?"* Hanani replied, *"The walls are still broken down, and the gates are burned with fire."* How is that relatable to us? We do not live in walled cites. It is relatable to us in the sense it speaks to the issue that there are specific boundaries and specific protections we need to have in our lives. If they are not right we become vulnerable. We become open to all sorts of problems—even enemy attack.

Some of us have the wrong kind of walls in our lives. We box everybody out. We do not want to risk relationships where we might get hurt. That is not what I am talking about. I am talking about, for instance, walls of *character*. That is certainly a wall we need to have in our lives. God wants to build character. He wants to help us develop the ability to make good decisions along godly lines.

It has to do with integrity and honesty. It's a moral compass that is put in place by God. When character is strong, it represents a solid wall in your life. But when character begins to weaken, we become vulnerable to all of the problems in this world, all of the things that are floating out in the ethos and the cosmos, things that ruin lives and destroy people.

A strong wall of *character* is of critical importance. *"Like a city whose walls are broken down is a man who lacks self-control."* — Proverbs 25:28 (NIV)

We need walls of *commitment*. Each of us needs to build commitment into our lives. We all know some things are more important than others, so we must use discernment to make solid decisions. "What am I going to spend my time doing?" We cannot simply wait for things to happen. We have to be proactive.

I think one vital commitment is to connect with a good church. We absolutely need that wall in our lives. When you are connected and committed to a local church you are part of a group designed to help build one another up so you can be stronger as you go back out into the world. The more you separate yourself, isolate yourself, remove yourself, you are distancing yourself from a source of great strength.

We need walls of personal *conviction*. These are the things we hold as our values. They define us. *"The walls are broken down. The gates are burned with fire."* This speaks to the fact that sometimes individuals get into situations where their character has been compromised, where they are not as committed to the things that are important as they ought to be, and where they are not living according to godly convictions.

Do you see how I'm using the term *walls*? Do you understand the significance? Are there times in your life when you feel like your walls have been broken down, where it has been like open season on you with temptation? If so, it is time for you to rebuild those walls. You are rebuilding the good things, the things that guard your heart and guard your life.

That was Nehemiah's focus. His intent was to change things dramatically.

On January 30, 1933, just before America inaugurated

Flour Power

President Franklin D. Roosevelt to his first term, German president Paul von Hindenburg was persuaded by some on his staff that they could control a former Austrian corporal named Adolf Hitler.

So he made Hitler Chancellor of Germany, thinking it would be mostly a symbolic role for the Nazi leader.

But sadly, history tells us that it took a mere 52 days before all of the political entities and bodies in that nation gave, by vote, Adolf Hitler absolute dictatorial power in Germany, and we know exactly what happened as a result of that.

Fifty-two days. A short period of time can make a real difference. It all depends on things like focus, vision, goals, commitment, and—yes—a sense of urgency.

In Nehemiah's world, we see another period of 52 days. But these became the backdrop for one of the greatest moments recorded in scripture.

The first step in all real change is to let the things that *should* bother you bother you and not let the things bother you that should not bother you. It is all about perspective. Too much of life is spent getting upset about all the wrong things. We all do it. We get bothered out of proportion to the seriousness and scope of problems. We get annoyed. We allow ourselves to become preoccupied.

I've called this chapter *The Bothered Butler* because often it takes getting upset for good things to begin happening. Nehemiah had to be bothered before he could have his breakthrough. Look at an oyster inside its shell. All it will ever be good for is for someone to harvest the oyster, take it to a restaurant, crack it open, add some hot sauce and some horseradish, maybe put it on a saltine and serve it to you, unless some sand gets into the shell and it gets hurt and irritated. Do you know what happens then?

A pearl.

Sometimes the things that annoy us and irritate us can result in vital changes in our lives. That is exactly what happened to Nehemiah. He said, "How's it going back there in Jerusalem?" And he heard the answer, "Not good." It hit him like a ton of bricks, so he proceeded to take those bricks, brick by brick, and do something about it. He knew the potential of tapping into the power of *sanctified mourning*. That is not just mourning, not just being sad, it is so much more than that.

Lots of things make us sad. The weather. Health concerns. Politics. What bothers you? What makes you sad? Some have truly learned how to mourn, they have lost loved ones and friends. Sadness and mourning are real. We all understand mourning.

But what about *sanctified mourning*? That happens when something hits us, and it makes us so sad it becomes a preoccupation, an obsession, and because we have the capacity to mourn in a sanctified way, it becomes an agent of change in our lives. The Book of James talks about it this way:

"Submit yourselves, then, to God. Resist the devil, and he will flee from you. Come near to God and he will come near to you. Wash your hands, you sinners, and purify your hearts, you double-minded." See the language? *"Grieve, mourn and wail. Change your laughter to mourning and your joy to gloom. Humble yourselves before the Lord, and he will lift you up."* — James 4:7-10 (NIV)

That is what Nehemiah did. We learn that as soon as he heard the bad news, he wept. He mourned. He fasted and prayed. Please understand Nehemiah was deeply broken, but the good news is that God can work with a crushed heart. The psalmist said, *"A broken and contrite heart, God, you will not despise."* (Psalm 51:17 NIV)

What bothers *you*?

When the apostle Paul went to Athens, he saw the whole city given over to idolatry. He had what is called in the Greek language a *paroxysm*. In other words, he freaked out. His heart broke for the people of Athens. It grieved him deeply. He had to do something about it, so he went to Mars Hill and preached about Jesus and the resurrection.

Are we immune to the problems around us? Great transformation happens in our lives when we become so bothered about what needs to be changed that we act. If we can take it or leave it, we will most likely leave it. But when something really grips us to the point that we think, "I must do something about this; I must solve this problem; I must change this issue," *then* change can happen in a powerful way.

According to that passage from the Book of James, there are four things sanctified mourning involves:

First, sanctified mourning involves *total surrender to God*.

Douglas MacArthur's 1945 return to the Philippines in World War II was a pivotal moment. He had left in early 1942 to go to Australia under presidential orders, famously saying, "I came through, and *I shall return.*" That became his mantra. In early 1945, he finally waded ashore at Leyte Beach. He called on the people to rally to him, and it was the beginning of the end for the enemy.

Do you remember what the terms of World War II were? Do you recall the stated goal of the Allies over the Axis powers whether it was the Germans in Europe or the Japanese in the Pacific? It was *unconditional surrender*. We do not use such terms anymore. We like negotiation. Some people even love to negotiate with God. "All right, God. You do this, and I'll do that. I'll meet you halfway."

Wrong.

We will never experience long-term spiritual life change

until we realize God's terms are always the same: unconditional, complete, absolute surrender.

What else does sanctified mourning involve? *Spiritual warfare.*

"Resist the Devil, and he will flee." When we mourn, we realize we are in a battle. There is a reason bad things happen. There is a reason the city needs walls. There are enemies. Your great enemy, your adversary... Peter doesn't say *the* adversary or *God's* adversary. He says *your.* Think of the Devil as your personal adversary.

"Be self-controlled and alert. Your enemy the devil prowls around like a roaring lion looking for someone to devour. Resist him, standing firm in the faith, because you know that your brothers throughout the world are undergoing the same kind of suffering." — I Peter 5:8-9 (NIV)

Sanctified mourning also involves *intimacy with God.* He says, "Draw near to me, and I will draw near to you." You may think, "But you said it wasn't a negotiation." That is not a negotiation. That is a challenge. You could spend all of your life waiting for God to come close to you and miss this point.

There was a 70's song that said, *"Darling, if you want me to be closer to you, get closer to me."* If you want to get closer to God and you want God to be closer to you, he says, "Draw near to me, and I will draw near to you." He does not say, "I will draw near to you, and then you'll see how cool that is, and you'll start coming my way." He already drew near to all of us when Jesus was on the cross. Can you do any better than that? Is there any greater love than a man laying down his life for his friends? Of course not, but we have to take that step to have intimacy with God.

Finally, sanctified mourning means *honesty with God*.

Here is the crux of the matter. Nehemiah was just an average person in an important job. He was a butler. He was not a prophet. He was not a pastor. He was not a priest. He was not even someone who grew up in Jerusalem and missed hanging out in the old "hood." He was simply someone who knew his heritage. God gripped his soul with a sense of burden, an idea he could not shake, a call he could not ignore and he made a difference in the world around him.

A compelling spiritual future comes when we let God do something in us so we can make a difference in the world around us. And it usually begins with getting upset enough to take ownership of a problem.

Nehemiah—the bothered butler—made a difference.

GOT ANY RIVERS?
Obstacles are Opportunities in Disguise

The first man to come up with the big idea was Charles V, Holy Roman Emperor and King of Spain back in 1534. Two hundred-fifty years later, Thomas Jefferson mused about it. Several decades later, a British company explored the idea, but nothing came of it. Then came the French, and they actually started work on the big idea. But then again, they had some experience in such things, seeing as they had been successful with a similar project in the Middle East, one originally suggested by a dreamer named Napoleon. But the French, after a noble effort, bailed out as the nineteenth century was getting ready to give way to its successor.

The big idea was to dig a passageway—a canal across the isthmus of what is now Panama. This would connect the Atlantic and Pacific oceans and save ships a boatload (sorry about that) of time by not having to go around that pesky continent of South America.

Finally, it was during the administration of the American president Theodore Roosevelt that the big idea began its transformation into reality. But of course, Teddy was a visionary who saw American might and ingenuity as boundless. The manmade waterway was opened in August 1914, and these days nearly 15,000 vessels take the shortcut each year.

It was a massive project, and toward the end the Americans became enamored of a little chorus they would sing while at work. The song's lyrics included the line: "we do things that are impossible, we do things other people can't do." Soon the words made their way into popular culture and advertising in the 1920s and 1930s.

Oscar C. Eliason was a young preacher in Minnesota who was recovering from a life-threatening illness in 1931. One day he came across an advertisement for a local construction company in a Minneapolis newspaper, one that included the lines from the old canal chorus: "We can do things that others cannot do, we do the impossible." Eliason believed that he had been touched and healed by God and that only God could do the impossible. Inspired, he put some words together and created a little chorus that began to be used in churches around Minnesota, eventually making its way to other parts of the country.

There's an interesting story from the early days of the Second World War about the song. A former Bible college student who had volunteered for the Army Air Corps was flying a practice run over Stockton, California and somehow his radio microphone got stuck open while he was singing this chorus. The testimony was given that several people down on the ground who heard this were convicted by it and eventually opened their hearts to Jesus Christ. This story was picked up by the Gideon's International. Eventually this powerful chorus became a staple for the Youth for Christ movement that came into being right after the war was over in the 1940s, just as Billy Graham was beginning to preach to thousands.

I became acquainted with the chorus when I was a child, but my favorite memories of it are from my Bible College days in Springfield, Missouri. While studying for the ministry, I attended the High Street Baptist Church, where Dr. David A. Cavin was pastor. He was a great old-school preacher, and he always remembered my name. I remember that about him. His church had thousands of members, but he always remembered my name.

And I was *very* forgettable.

Like many of the old-time preachers, Dr. Cavin would occasionally break into song right in the middle of his message. It was charming, even if the man really could not sing. Not a lick. He had a gravelly voice I can still hear him trying his very best to sing this chorus:

> *"Got any rivers you think are uncrossable?*
> *Got any mountains you cannot tunnel through?*
> *God specializes in things thought impossible,*
> *He can do things others cannot do."*

Got any issues in your life that are difficult—in fact, so challenging that you think they can never be resolved? Got any mountains that loom large in your path and you just can't figure a work-around? Well, there is good news—God specializes in such things. The Bible is filled with dramatic accounts of how God has intervened in time and space to solve complex human problems. The children of Israel came to the Red Sea—a seemingly impossible and uncrossable barrier. But not to God—He specializes in the impossible. The water divided and a divine highway appeared, paved with delivering grace.

Later, these same people needed food. So God sent them the original wonder bread—manna from Heaven. They needed water, so God turned a solid rock into a refreshing fountain. And along the journey through history, when people of faith found themselves facing walls, those barriers fell down. When they were threatened by hungry lions, the beasts were miraculously tamed.

All because God specializes in things thought impossible.

One of my favorite stories in the Bible about this kind of deliverance, when God showed up in a desperate situation, is found in the book of Second Kings in the Old Testament. It was during a period of cultural decline for the nation of Israel, as they were sliding toward judgment. By this time—many generations after the reign of King David, and then his son Solomon the kingdom was divided. The Northern Kingdom—referred to as Israel—was perpetually apostate, yet there were moments when the people bore witness to the great grace of God. The Southern Kingdom is known as Judah. They fared somewhat better than their counterpart in the north as far as spiritual values was concerned, but still fell far short of their past glory and fellowship with God.

Now at this moment in time Ahab's youngest son Joram was reigning, and they were perpetually being harassed by their enemies, particularly the Syrians. The situation was perilous:

Some time later, Ben-Hadad king of Aram mobilized his entire army and marched up and laid siege to Samaria. There was a great famine in the city; the siege lasted so long that a donkey's head sold for eighty shekels of silver, and a quarter of a cab of seed pods for five shekels.

As the king of Israel was passing by on the wall, a woman cried to him, "Help me, my lord the king!"

The king replied, "If the Lord does not help you, where can I get help for you? From the threshing floor? From the winepress?" Then he asked her, "What's the matter?"

She answered, "This woman said to me, 'Give up your son so we may eat him today, and tomorrow we'll eat my son.' So we cooked my son and ate him. The next day I said to her, 'Give up your son so we may eat him,' but she had hidden him."

When the king heard the woman's words, he tore his robes. As he went along the wall, the people looked, and they saw that, under his robes, he had sackcloth on his body. He said, "May God deal with me, be it ever so severely, if the head of Elisha son of Shaphat remains on his shoulders today!"

Now Elisha was sitting in his house, and the elders were sitting with him. The king sent a messenger ahead, but before he arrived, Elisha said to the elders, "Don't you see how this murderer is sending someone to cut off my head? Look, when the messenger comes, shut the door and hold it shut against him. Is not the sound of his master's footsteps behind him?" While he was still talking to them, the messenger came down to him.

The king said, "This disaster is from the Lord. Why should I wait for the Lord any longer?" — II Kings 6:24-33 (NIV)

My wife and I visited St. Petersburg, Russia a few years ago, which was called Leningrad during the Second World War. It is a city notable for a great siege at the hands of Nazi Germany—one that lasted more than a thousand days during the conflict the Russians still refer to as "The Great Patriotic War." Supply lines were cut. People suffered and starved. A siege is a brutal tactic in warfare.

So the city of Samaria was under siege. They didn't have any food. The siege lasted so long that a donkey's

Flour Power

head sold for eighty shekels of silver. That's roughly two pounds of silver. Now I want you to think about that. Today, we price silver by the ounce, so they had to pay thirty-two ounces for a donkey's head. If you wanted a nice "DLT" (donkey, lettuce, and tomato), you had to dig deep. But you couldn't, because no one had any money. And there was no bread, not to mention lettuce and tomato. And forget about the mayo.

How did they feel? How would *you* feel?

Whether your problem is big or small, whether it's a family problem, a personal problem, a neighborhood problem, a work problem, a cultural problem, or a national problem—the response is the same. We soon feel overwhelmed. These problems become insurmountable, like rivers we cannot cross, and mountains we cannot tunnel through.

Paralyzed. Hopeless. No way out. We're all going to die!

Got any rivers?

People are capable of the unthinkable during desperate times. One day the king was walking on the wall of the city, giving him a vantage point to observe the situation. His attention was drawn to an escalating argument between two young women. He decided to intervene. He asked them about the nature of their conflict. One woman said: "We decided, we agreed that we would boil my child and eat it one day then her child the next day."

That's how bad it had gotten.

The king was shocked. He put on sackcloth and ashes—symbolizing humility and prayer.

He was also angry.

He was not just angry at the Syrians, he was angry at God for letting this happen. And he focused that anger on a preacher named Elisha.

Elisha was a prophet of God and a man of influence in the realm. He was the "kinder-gentler" successor to Elijah—a man of shock and awe. But while he may have had a different temperament than his polarizing predecessor, Elisha was a formidable man in his own right.

The king was so mad that he wanted to see Elisha dead. He wanted the preacher's head by sundown.

Meanwhile, Elisha was meeting with a group of city leaders. God reveals the king's threat to him and he tells the men around him that the king and his emissary are on their way to do him bodily harm.

Got any rivers?

Flour Power

Desperate problems should drive us to dynamic promises. Whenever you have a problem, seek the corresponding promise. There is a promise from God in the Bible for every problem you have. He wants to show it to you—but you must be open to His leadership in your life.

They needed some hope during that terrible siege. They needed somebody to tell them that there could be some good news. So when Elisha confronts the king who wants his head on a platter, here's what happens:

Elisha replied, "Hear the word of the Lord. This is what the Lord says: About this time tomorrow, a seah of the finest flour will sell for a shekel and two seahs of barley for a shekel at the gate of Samaria." — II Kings 7:1 (NIV)

God would deliver—sooner, not later. By this time tomorrow. Food. Lots of it. On sale, too. Piece of cake. Or anything you want to make with all the flour you will be able to buy for your family. It's a promise from God—delivered by His servant. A preacher of hope.

God may not speak to us directly today the way He did to and through Elisha, but He does speak to us through His Word. Are you struggling with how to make ends meet in this day and age? Well, what does He say? There's a promise, Philippians 4:19 *"My God will meet all your needs according to the riches of his glory in Christ Jesus."* 'I feel so small compared to my problems.'

Philippians 4:13- *"I can do all things through Christ who strengthens me."* 'I'm so filled with anxiety.' *"Seek ye first the kingdom of God and his righteousness and all of these things shall be taken care of, added unto you."* (Matthew 6:33) There's a promise for your problem. You got a problem with the flesh and your weaknesses? *"Walk in the Spirit and you shall not fulfill the lust of the flesh."* — Galatians 5:16

The Apostle Peter referred to them as *"very great and precious promises."* (II Peter 1:4)

When you're in a desperate moment, when there's a river you cannot cross, when there's a mountain you cannot tunnel through, you need to find out what the word of the Lord says. Find out what God is saying about the situation. God's promises are always fulfilled. We don't always keep our promises, people break their promises all the time. Promises are broken in every political campaign, but God never breaks a promise. Desperate problems should drive us to dynamic promises.

Got any rivers?

God's grace works best through human weakness. This is an important point. Did you ever wonder why God will allow you to go through stuff that really beats you down? Because when we are weak we are most capable of tapping into the power of God.

Flour Power

God *does not* want to be your co-pilot.

Have you ever seen that bumper sticker, "God is my co-pilot?" Well, what is He doing in the *second* seat? He should be flying the whole plane. He should own the airline. He owns the air. Copilot? Nope.

When I was a kid there was a popular hair cream. My dad used to put it on his hair, and I put it on my hair. It was called *Brylcreem*. They had a TV commercial for the stuff. And they had a famous slogan: *"A little dab'll do ya."*

Well, many preachers, my father included, saw that as too great an illustration to pass up. So you'd hear things from the pulpit like: "My friends, some of you don't want to fully surrender to God. When it comes to the things of the Lord, you just want *Brylcreem* religion—a little dab'll do ya."

Cultural relevance in the mid-1960s.

Of course, it's true. Some want to be sermon samplers and spiritual food tasters, but they stop short at really digging in and experiencing God's full banquet of blessings. A little Easter and a little Christmas, that's all they need. That is, until something beats them down—or up. Then God has this way of taking the weakness and turning it into strength. Infirmity can become the catalyst for great deliverance.

Now there were four men with leprosy at the entrance of the city gate. They said to each other, "Why stay here until we die? If we say, 'We'll go into the city'—the famine is there, and we will die. And if we stay here, we will die. So let's go over to the camp of the Arameans and surrender. If they spare us, we live; if they kill us, then we die." — II Kings 7:4-5 (NIV)

Weak men. Desperate men. Hurting men. Unlikely heroes.

They were outside the city because they were outcasts and couldn't be inside because their disease was both highly contagious and seriously stigmatized. Leprosy was a major blight in the ancient world. God used it in scripture as a metaphor for what sin does to the soul. It's a picture of sin, and so a leper was unclean, as we are spiritually unclean without Jesus.

These four leprous guys are outside the city. They're in between the camp of the enemy and the besieged city.

Our two oldest grandkids got us roped into watching "The Walking Dead." Every time I read this passage in the Bible I think these four leprous men must have looked like the walking dead. Just hideous and covered with all kinds of sores.

But these are the people God often decides to use to make all the difference. God will choose the foolish to confound the wise every time.

Never underestimate something small. Remember

when the crowd listening to Jesus got hungry and the only solution seemed absurd—a boy giving his small lunch to Jesus? Never underestimate the insignificant; never underestimate that small thing. It could be a young person. It could be four lepers.

Got any rivers?

Followers of Jesus are, by definition, supernaturalists. We are surrounded by the supernatural. When someone really "gets" this truth, it can be life-changing —even world changing. Moses, for example: *"By faith he left Egypt, not fearing the king's anger; he persevered because he saw Him who is invisible."* —Hebrews 11:27 (NIV)

The Bible talks a lot about the spiritual warfare in high places and the supernatural angels.

There's a story earlier in the life of Elisha where some enemies were coming after him. His personal assistant freaked out.

When the servant of the man of God got up and went out early the next morning, an army with horses and chariots had surrounded the city. "Oh no, my lord! What shall we do?" the servant asked. "Don't be afraid," the prophet answered. "Those who are with us are more than those who are with them." And Elisha prayed, "Open his eyes, Lord, so that he may see." Then the Lord opened the servant's eyes, and he looked and saw the hills full of horses and chariots of fire all around Elisha. —II Kings 6:15-17 (NIV)

It reminds me of the old boxing story about the guy who's getting soundly beaten by the other guy. He staggers back to his corner and is treated for cuts—he's a bloody mess. His manager is trying to encourage him: "You got him right where you want him, he hasn't laid a glove on you. You're winning this thing." Of course, this wasn't the case at all. Finally the fighter says: "Okay, I'll go back out and give it my best, but someone keep an eye on that referee, because someone in that ring is hurtin' me bad."

Elisha prays *"Open his eyes Lord, so that he may see."* Then the assistant saw the unseen. He saw the supernatural.

One of the greatest lessons to learn again and again in life is to pray: *"Lord, I feel overwhelmed, I don't think I can make it. Please open my eyes so that I can see and perceive your supernatural power. So that I can sense your presence."*

Those four leprous men were part of the puzzle. That was the human part—the weak part. Now all that was needed was God's supernatural strength.

At dusk they got up and went to the camp of the Arameans. When they reached the edge of the camp, no one was there, for the Lord had caused the Arameans to hear the sound of chariots and horses and a great army, so that they said to one another, "Look, the king of Israel has hired the Hittite and Egyptian kings to attack us!" So they got up and fled in the dusk and abandoned their tents and their horses and donkeys. They left the camp as it was and ran for their lives. — II Kings 7:5-7 (NIV)

God just caused a gigantic noise. It was like a large fighting force of warriors on horseback coming up the road. These are professional military men. They know the sound of an army approaching. God crafted this supernatural noise.

We live in a noisy world. I don't know if we can fully appreciate this. I remember reading years ago about the Lewis and Clark expedition across the country and how when they got within several miles of the Pacific Ocean they could actually hear the waves crashing because there was no ambient noise. The sounds of modernity had not touched that spot, yet.

This noise was paralyzing and it shook the men besieging the city. It was very real to them. And they got out of there.

So the lepers went into the ghost camp. They went from tent to tent. There was food, drink, clothing, armor, and provisions. Just think about how giddy they must have been. Hungry, empty, at the point of death and desperation. It had to be awesome!

Got any rivers?

Have you ever heard the wise saying: "Hurting people hurt people?" In other words, wounded people can be filled with such inner conflict that they wind up, ironically, inflicting pain on others. And often they feel justified, if not clueless.

Well, the opposite of that is found in the next part of this story: "Blessed people should bless people."

The men who had leprosy reached the edge of the camp, entered one of the tents and ate and drank. Then they took silver, gold and clothes, and went off and hid them. They returned and entered another tent and took some things from it and hid them also. Then they said to each other, "What we're doing is not right. This is a day of good news and we are keeping it to ourselves. If we wait until daylight, punishment will overtake us. Let's go at once and report this to the royal palace." —II Kings 7:8-9 (NIV)

These desperate men had a moment of clarity and conviction. This, in turn, led to ultimate fulfillment of Elisha's bold prophecy. I suppose there is no need to belabor this point. When God blesses, when He delivers, when He intervenes and helps, it is not just for us—it is for others in our sphere of influence.

Don't be a reservoir, just hoarding God's favor. Be a river—let Him flow His many blessings through you toward others.

One of the things I love about the church I've had the privilege to lead since 1998—Expectation Church in Fairfax, Virginia—is that the congregation is not striving to keep everyone the same and just have a happy community while we wait for Jesus to come back. Not at all. Like the church at Antioch (Acts 13), we rejoice when God removes people from us and takes them to other places to serve. Church planting is a big part of our ministry vision.

Our local church recently sent a team to the San Francisco Bay area in California to start a new church. No easy field. These servants of the Lord are taking a little DNA from us with them. Why? Because the world is sick and dying—and we have the cure. These servants of the Lord have the cure in their hearts—the person and work of Jesus Christ. It's in them, it flows through their spiritual veins. They've had a day of good news. They've been delivered from their spiritual leprosy. They've been fed, they've been equipped and they're going to go out to a little fledgling laboratory out there in the San Francisco area and start spreading the cure.

They're not trying to figure out what the cure is. They have it. But they have to find effective delivery mechanisms to make ministry effective in that cultural context.

Not everybody will take the cure. Some won't believe its real. But others will, and they will be made whole. Then they will become new workers in the laboratory (local church) and the efforts will be multiplied.

There's a French phrase called "noblesse oblige." It means "the obligation of the nobility." The idea is that people who were born to money or privilege have a moral obligation to do things for people who are less fortunate. We, as the blessed children of God, have a moral obligation to bless others. We have the cure.

Got any rivers?

When it comes to categorizing sin—ranking bad behavior—too many people leave out one of the most serious ways we fall short of the glory of God.

Unbelief.

Unbelief is serious sin. Earlier, I mentioned how Elisha stood up in the city gate and promised that in about twenty-four hours the besieged and desperate populace would be able to buy groceries at bargain basement prices.

That's when the king's assistant—think of him as a self-important guy with a clipboard—had this exchange with the preacher: *"Look, even if the Lord should open the floodgates of the heavens, could this happen? You will see it with your own eyes," answered Elisha, "but you will not eat any of it!"* —II Kings 7:2 (NIV)

Floodgates of heaven.

That is an interesting characterization. The only time prior to this that the floodgates of heaven are mentioned is in Genesis in reference to the great flood in Noah's day. Then later on, in the final book of the Old Testament, there is a reference to the floodgates— also known as the "windows of heaven"—as a reference to the outpouring of God's blessings.

The metaphor about something big coming from heaven morphs from a description of judgment to one of abundance.

Elisha's rebuke of the king's assistant was abrupt and brutal. I find the whole "Elisha vs. Elijah" thing fascinating—because too many people rush to judgment. Usually it goes something like this: "Elijah? Well, he was a bold prophet. Pulled no punches. Didn't mince words. A ready-fire-aim kind of preacher. But Elisha? Well, he was gentle, more relational, not as prone to offend or antagonize." But such analysis falls short of what the scriptures actually describe. Elisha had the capacity for boldness and "Elijah-like" pronouncements.

And one thing that really pushed Elisha's indignation button was unbelief, because the man of God knew that it was a grievous sin.

It still is.

The writer of the New Testament Book of Hebrews reflected on how the sin of unbelief—a lack of faith at a crucial moment in history—led to the generational failure of the Exodus generation:

See to it, brothers and sisters, that none of you has a sinful, unbelieving heart that turns away from the living God. But encourage one another daily, as long as it is called "Today," so that none of you may be hardened by sin's deceitfulness. We have come to share in Christ, if indeed we hold our original conviction firmly to the very end. As has just been said:

*"Today, if you hear his voice,
do not harden your hearts
as you did in the rebellion."*

Who were they who heard and rebelled? Were they not all those Moses led out of Egypt? And with whom was he angry for forty years? Was it not with those who sinned, whose bodies perished in the wilderness? And to whom did God swear that they would never enter his rest if not to those who disobeyed? So we see that they were not able to enter, because of their unbelief. — Hebrews 3:12-19 (NIV)

Unbelief can rear its ugly head in many forms. Some may think of themselves as "realists." Others as "cynics" or "skeptics." And there are moments in our lives when a measure of skepticism can be healthy and helpful. But only when dealing with people and their promises—not when dealing with God and His promises.

"…in the hope of eternal life, which <u>God, who does not lie</u>, promised before the beginning of time…" —Titus 1:2 (NIV)

The great moment comes—the moment of fulfillment. God has providentially provided. Food is available in abundance. And at a great price—no coupons needed.

And the king's assistant—the self-important guy with the clipboard—jumps on the bandwagon. These days we call this a "flip-flop." His previous statement is "no longer operative." He doesn't want to be left out of the big moment. So he takes charge.

He stood in the city gate with his clipboard and told everyone to line up and be orderly. He was in charge, and he insisted that people listen and follow his instructions. But his clipboard was no match for a mob of mothers who needed food for their families.

Now the king had put the officer on whose arm he leaned in charge of the gate, and the people trampled him in the gateway, and he died, just as the man of God had foretold when the king came down to his house. It happened as the man of God had said to the king: "About this time tomorrow, a seah of the finest flour will sell for a shekel and two seahs of barley for a shekel at the gate of Samaria."

The officer had said to the man of God, "Look, even if the Lord should open the floodgates of the heavens, could this happen?" The man of God had replied, "You will see it with your own eyes, but you will not eat any of it!" And that is exactly what happened to him, for the people trampled him in the gateway, and he died. —II Kings 7:17-20 (NIV)

This man saw the blessing but he did not receive it. You might say, "Oh that poor guy. That's an awful story. It doesn't seem fair that he was trampled." But when we refuse to believe the promises of God we are always going to miss out on God's best. And there will be times when it will seem that those true believers running the good race for the Lord will overrun us if we don't get out of the way.

I don't delight in the demise of the man who trusted his clipboard more than the promises of God. But it reminds me that faith in God's promises will make all the difference. And unbelief anytime will lead to God's judgment. So when I have a problem, I look for His promise. That's how I can see God do the impossible.

Got any rivers you think are uncrossable?
Got any mountains you cannot tunnel through?
God specializes in things thought impossible.
He can do things others cannot do.

ACKNOWLEDGEMENTS

Special thanks to Tracey Dowdy, my editorial assistant, for her excellent work shaping this book. I pray that she will never grow weary of having to plod through my prose on a daily basis. She helps make my words readable.

Eowyn Riggins, our graphic designer, is relatively new to our team, but she has already proven herself to be a wonderful creative force. She designed this book's cover.

Flour Power is based on a talk I shared on a Sunday morning with the Expectation Church family a while back. One of our members—in fact, the Chairman of our church Fellowship of Deacons—created a poem from the notes he took that day. Reverend Howard "Ike" Hendershot has a flair for verse, and I've included his take on *Flour Power* at the beginning of the book. Ike is retired from the United States Secret Service, and recently served as President of the Association of Former Agents U. S. Service. He currently serves as a chaplain for the Fairfax County Polices Department.

Finally, I remain, as always, grateful to Karen—the love of my life and my best friend. We have now been on this journey together for more than 40 wonderful years. And I never cease to be amazed at her patience with me, particularly when I am driven to distraction in the writing zone. Together we have seen *Flour Power* work powerfully in our lives so many times down through the years.

David R. Stokes
Senior Pastor of Expectation Church
Fairfax, Virginia
December 2016

ABOUT THE AUTHOR

DAVID R. STOKES is an ordained minister, bestselling author, commentator, broadcaster, and columnist. He's been married to the love of his life, Karen, for 40 years. They have three daughters and seven grandchildren. And they all live in the great and beautiful Commonwealth of Virginia. David's website is: www.davidrstokes.com.

Made in the USA
Lexington, KY
18 December 2016